Fingerstyle for Beginners

Simple Fingerpicking Songbook and TAB

Video tutorials that accompany this songbook
are available seperately at andyguitar.co.uk

EASY FINGERSTYLE
FOR BEGINNERS

This series of lessons teaches simple melodies and songs at the same time as Finger picking technique. It can be done even by total beginners.

However, it is best for those who have experience playing chord based songs and strumming, but who need more experience playing single note melodies before moving on to intermediate and advanced fingerstyle playing.

This is the ideal precursor to my intermediate fingerstyle course where we'll learn how to play chord & melody song arrangements along with finger picking patterns at a higher level.

CONTENTS

This course contains simple melody only arrangements of the following songs:

1. Hot Crossed Buns
2. Happy Birthday
3. Amazing Grace
4. For He's a Jolly Good Fellow
5. Greensleeves
6. Ode To Joy
7. Twinkle Twinkle
8. Oh Danny Boy
9. Swing low Sweet Chariot
10. Canon in D
11. Danse Macabre
12. Minuet in G

Help with reading Tab is given in with every song. Chord symbols are also included where appropriate.

Here's a super simple melody to get you started. It's also an opportunity to get used to reading guitar TAB (short for Tablature)

Here's our first simple song, Hot Crossed Buns. It's worth checking that you understand how to play this melody fully and understand how it is written before moving on to some of the more popular pieces in this course.

Hot Crossed Buns

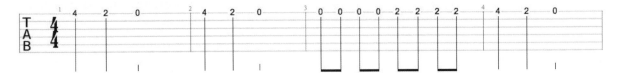

Reading TAB
The numbers above show the fret numbers you should play on which string. We choose which finger we use depending on the situation.

The video that accompanies this lesson shows which finger to use to play each note.

Reading rhythms in TAB
Not all guitar TAB shows rhythms, but each TAB in this course does.

The first two notes (written '4' and '2') last one beats,
known as a Quarter Note as it lasts a quarter of the bar.

The third note (written 0') lasts two beats,
known as a Half Note as it lasts half a bar.

2 - Happy Birthday

Happy Birthday is the most well known song on the planet, so it's well worth learning!

Happy Birthday

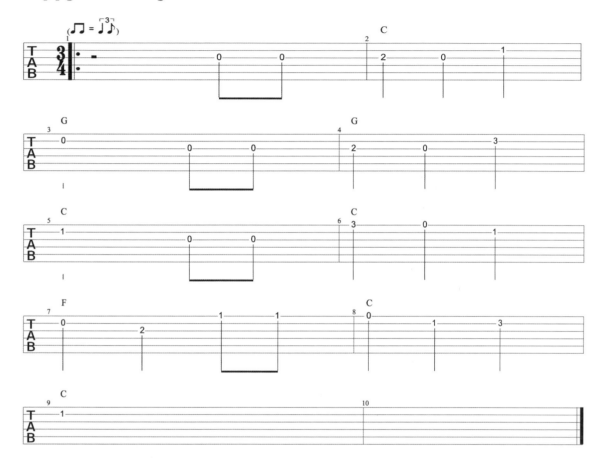

Getting the rhythm right

There is a jolly 'bounce' to this song, which is written in the TAB above the first bar. This shows that the 8th notes should all be played with this bounce or swing rhythm

In basic terms, this means play it to the rhythm that you would sing it - singing along will help!

3 - Amazing Grace

Amazing Grace is such a beautiful song. In the follow-on course to this, we look at how to play the chords at the same time as this melody, which is the gateway to higher level Fingerstyle guitar!

Amazing Grace

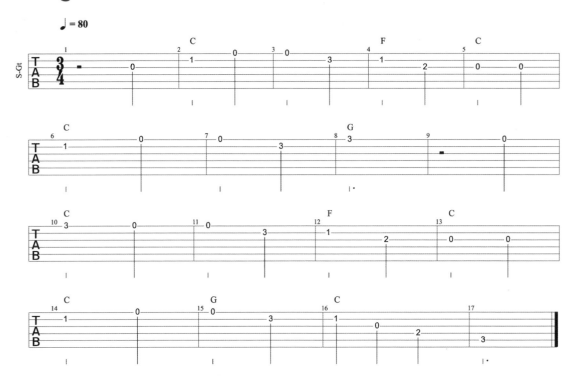

Chord symbols

The chords are written above each bar. This allows you to strum a simple version of this song and sing along if you wish. We'll learn how to play these same chords with the melody at the same time in my Intermediate Fingerstyle Course.

This melody is a little faster. It is a crucial stepping stone to increasing your speed with finger picking.

For He's A Jolly Good Fellow

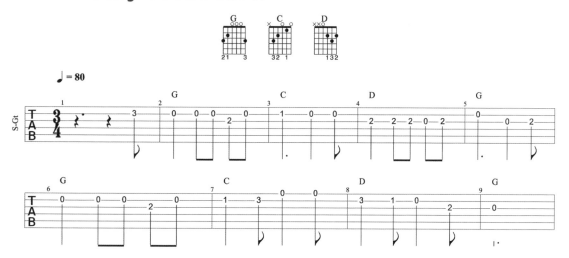

5 - Greensleeves

Greensleeves is a very old song and the sound of it evokes the time period of when it was written.

This is a longer piece, so it may take more time to learn. Work through it one line at a time and you will get it down.

Greensleeves

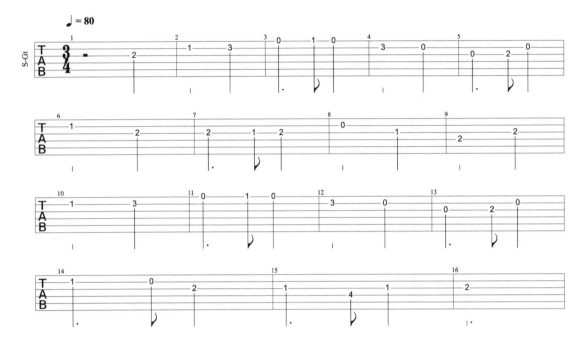

3:4 Time Signature

The 3 over 4 symbol at the start of the TAB tells us that there are three beats in a bar and that those beats are quarter notes. This song is therefore to a count of one, two, three, as opposed to counting to four beats per bar.

Ode To Joy is one of the most recognisable melodies in the world. Here, we'll learn the simply melody.

In the follow-on to this course, we'll look at how to add chords to this melody along with Travis Picking. Travis Picking is an alternating bass note played by the thumb, an intermediate level technique. More on bass notes on page 15.

Ode To Joy

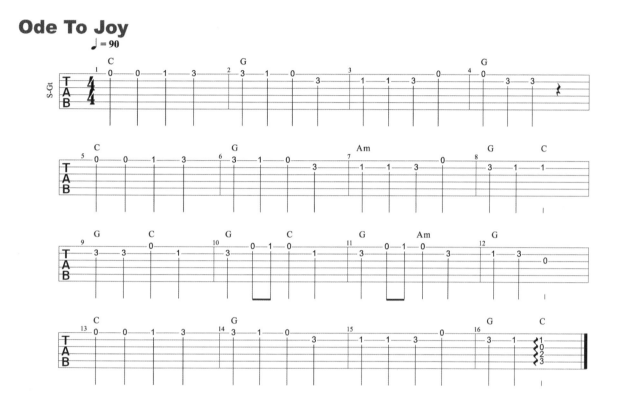

Chord symbols

The chords are written above each bar. This allows you to strum a simple version of this song and sing along if you wish.

Not the most 'Rock n Roll' of songs, but this is the best example of how the major scale can be used to create a simple melody that I know of, and that's why I've included it here.

Twinkle Twinkle

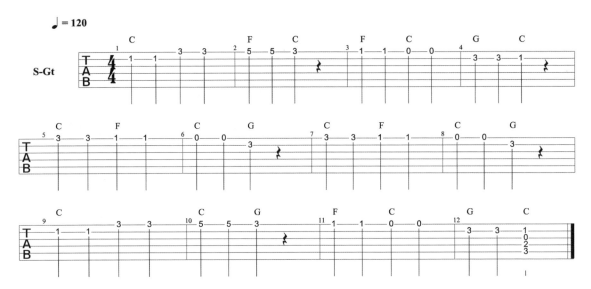

Chord symbols

Again, the chords are written above each bar. This allows you to strum a simple version of this song and sing along if you wish.

We'll learn how to play these same chords with the melody at the same time with Travis Picking in my Intermediate Fingerstyle Course.

8 - Oh Danny Boy

Here's one for the Irish, or those of Irish descent, or for those who appreciate a beautiful song when they hear one :)

Again, the chords are written above each bar. This allows you to strum a simple version of this song and sing along if you wish.

Oh Danny Boy

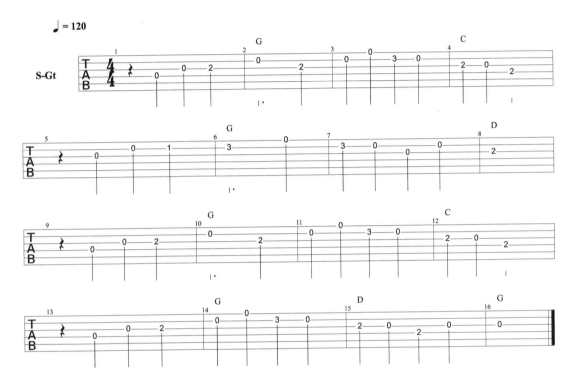

What's that squiggle at the start?
The first little squiggle in the TAB at the start of bar one is called a rest.

This just means don't play, and this particular squiggle indicates a one beat rest.

This one is a big Rugby anthem in the UK. It is known worldwide for many other reasons too.

This song, along with Danny Boy is in the key of G. This means it uses the G major scale for the melody and also uses the chords in the key of G, which include G major C major and D major, among others.

Swing Low Sweet Chariot

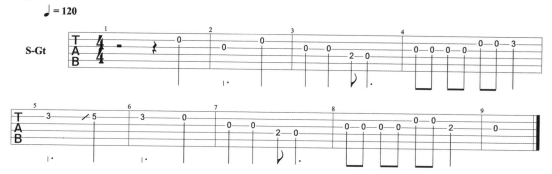

4:4 Time signature
The 4:4 symbol at the start of the TAB indicates that there are four beats in the bar. This means that each bar must add up to four beats, including the rest time values. This also means we count to four in each bar, like at the start of my Beginners Course (Level 1 Lesson 4!).

Rests
The first little squiggle in the TAB is called a rest. This just means 'don't play', and this particular squiggle indicates a one beat rest.

The little block at the start of this bar is a two beat rest. This is important because the note and rest values must add up to four beats in each bar.

This is one of the greatest classical pieces of all time. It has also been featured in a fair few viral YouTube videos over the past few years, just not by me sadly!

This is the first time in this course where we'll be adding a bass note and then chords. We do much more of this in my follow-on Fingerstyle Course. However, this is a perfect starting point for anyone wanting to go down this route in any style within the fingerpicking genre.

This will take longer than the rest to complete the TAB, but we'll start off super simple and layer it as we go.

Each line will have the same melody and even chords, we'll just start simple and add something extra on each new line.

Canon in D

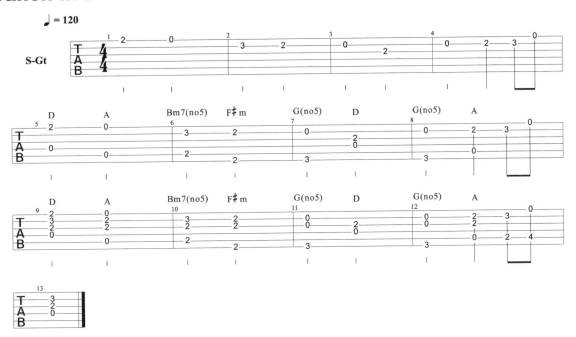

What is a 'bass note'?
A bass note aka root note is the lowest note of a chord. It also gives the chord it's name

i.e. D chord has a D root note - the open D string!

It can usually also played by the bass player in a band, but the same term is used to describe the lowest note in all guitar chords.

Scary chord names
There are some pretty scary looking chord names in the TAB for this one, but they are actually pretty easy to play i.e. no barre chords!

I love this song. I first heard it as the theme tune for the Jonathan Creek TV series here in the UK. It's dark and haunting but also beautiful.

The end bit is really tricky for most, but is a great example of how we can move up the neck in fingerstyle guitar while also keeping bass notes and chord tones ringing out under the melody!

Danse Macabre

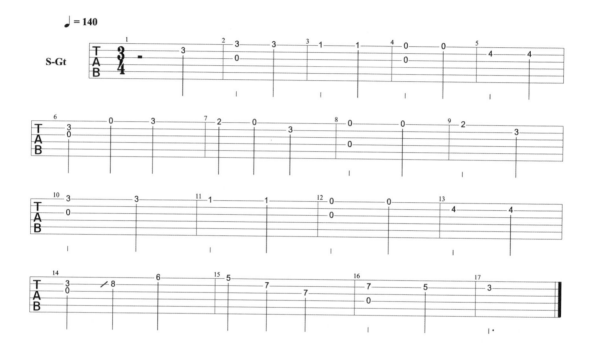

Slides in TAB
There is a slide written in bar 14 with the / symbol, which makes the move up the fretboard much easier and sound better. It can be really tricky to do this and requires a feel to really nail the slide, give it time and it will come and it will sound awesome!

Here's the final tune in this series. We're picking up the speed here!

This melody involves a run up and down the G major scale. It also involves a 'pattern' on the second line, which I explain more in the video.

Minuet in G

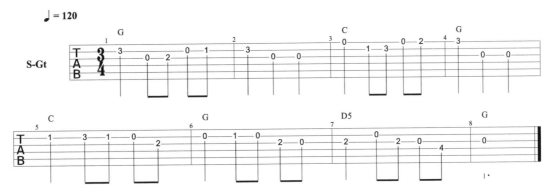

Major Scale Patterns

Learn more about 'patterns' with the major scale in my Acoustic Lead Guitar Course and also my Intermediate Guitar course, both are available at andyguitar.co.uk and on the Andy Guitar APP!

This course can be downloaded and streamed on the new Andy Guitar APP

Available now
on all iOS and Android devices

Andy's Intermediate Fingerstyle Course

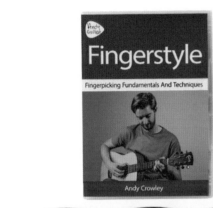

This is the direct follow on from this course you are looking at right now.

Andy's Intermediate Fingerstyle Course is available now in the following formats

3 DVD set and paperback book

Digital download + unlimited streaming on any device from andyguitar.co.uk

Also available on the Andy Guitar app!

Complete Andy Guitar Collection

Beginner Guitar Course

The flagship AndyGuitar product. Taking anyone from absolute beginner to knowing all the basic open chords, strumming patterns and scales needed to play 100s of easy songs. Practice routines and helpful tips given throughout!

Available as a download, 3 x DVD set and as a full colour 92 page paperback book and also as digital downloads.

Improver Guitar Course

The follow on from my beginners course. Covers how to play all barre chords and power chords. Also includes cheats and easier alternatives to each barre chord!

Complete with play along tracks to test and consolidate your skills!

Available as a download, 2 DVD + CD set and as a full colour 54 page paperback book and also as digital downloads.

Intermediate Guitar Course

Complete Andy's main syllabus with this direct follow on from the Beginners and Improver Courses. This is appropriate for Electric or Acoustic guitar. It covers rhythm and lead guitar techniques, scales and improvisation, strumming, chords and arpeggios, everything you need to give you the skills to be able to play litterally thousands of your favourite songs!

Consolidate your knowledge, refine your technique and learn how to truly be an intermediation going on advance guitarist in a number of genres!

Available at andyguitar.co.uk/shop and on Amazon

Beginner Strumming Course

Designed for those who need more help with strumming than my Beginner or Improver Courses provide. Includes a unique way for beginners to get to grips with rhythm and strumming. Also includes strumming patterns at a full intermediate level!

Available as a download, 2 DVD set and as a full colour 24 page paperback book and also as digital downloads

Rock Guitar 1 - Electric Starter Course

Want to get started with more Rock Guitar specific playing than my Beginners Course provides? Want to play along to rock songs right away and crank up the overdrive? Then this course is for you!

Rock Guitar 2 - Rock Rhythm Guitar

Available now on digital download & streaming only from andyguitar.co.uk. Includes 12 audio jam tracks to test your new rhythm guitar skills.

Rock Guitar 3 - Rock Lead Guitar

Learn all the essential Rock lead guitar techniques and licks, plus learn how to improvise and create your own solos! Includes 10 audio jam tracks to test your new lead guitar skills.

Easy Fingerstyle for Beginners

Learn all the essential Finger picking techniques plus how to read TAB with this in depth course. Includes 12 easy songs and melodies played without a pick using fingerpicking.

Intermediate Fingerstyle Course

This intermediate fingerstyle course gives a complete overveiw of all Finger Picking techniques inclding Travis picking, essential finger picking patterns and how to play a melody while adding chords on one guitar!

Available as a download, 3 DVD set and also full colour paperback songbook!

Available at andyguitar.co.uk/shop and on Amazon

Printed in Great Britain
by Amazon